Marred Days

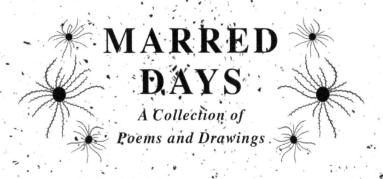

MARRED DAYS

A Collection of
Poems and Drawings

K. M. Jost

To you.

Table of Contents

Table of Contents

Table of Contents

Table of Contents

Daymare

/ˈdāmer/

Noun

> A frightening or oppressive trance or hallucinatory condition experienced while awake.

- Oxford Dictionary

K. M. Jost

The Thing in the Chair

There's a thing in the chair in the house
Where wood floors cover the earth.
The thing I see is just for me
In the corner of the wood floored house.

A beam of light falls through the window
The moon daring to show
The chair just sits and creaks a bit
As the light finds its way through.

My breathing heart fills the air
Heavy, chaotic, still fear.
No movement in sight is dead or asleep
The shadows pound in my ears.

I can now see it clear,
The thing in the chair in the house,
Shadows draping its frame, I can't help but gasp,
And now the thing knows I'm here.

It shifts in the seat.
I can't see its feet.

It has my eyes,
And it stares at me.
Brown,
Unblinkingly human.

Sparse wrong eyepatches of black fur,
Snout like a bear,
But the skin is wrinkled and old,
Diseased,
The fur extends where it can.

It grins at me from its chair where it sits.
Sharp,
Fangs dripping onto the floor.

So round and slow
And quick enough.
The paws are innocent,
Even cute.

But the paws wave me over,
Inviting.

I walk to the chair that never moves.

The floor is stained from the dripping.

I tried to get out of the house with wood floors
But the thing in the chair was precise.
It lives in that corner and waves in its prey
Who never leave the grip of the night.

The chair still creaks from time to time,
But muted and distant and far.
Moonlight won't reach here
It's too damp and dark
With the thing in the house in the chair.

Marred Days

On The Wall

The mirror on my wall is old.
It's warped and cracked along the edge.
When I'm alone it lets me through
If I wish to cross the ledge.

Into the wall

F
A
L
L

A Reflection of my backwards self becomes
The person I've implied.
I wonder if this is how Alice felt
when she got stuck on the other side.

Puddle

A harmless puddle in the street
Grabs ahold of children's feet
And sucks them

                 D

             o

                    W

                         n

                            b

                               e

                                   L

                                       O

                                          w

                                      .

The Sound Of

there was a noise
in the woods
as I was walking home

it was large and heavy
snapping twigs
as trees began to bend

a growl cried out
with a howl of pain
and I started to run

the wind picked up
breeze shifting
cold settling low to the ground

mist crawling in
breath weaving out
Closer and Closer and Closer

a chase in the dark
with an obvious winner
as the noise got louder each second

SNAP
　　CRUNCH
SNAP
　　CRUNCH

　　　　　　waUhEeeUe

　SNAP

B R E A K

a song of the end
carried by the dense fog
wandered its way into town

my cry was the wind
and that was the end
as the noise drifted back to the woods

Drop

It lives in the pipes
With sewage and mites
And waits 'til you turn on the tap

It plops out of the sink
And into your drink
To go down your throat through the gap

Once inside
It grows to a size
About as big as a bud

Then after a while
It chews through the bile
And drains your whole body of blood

Back in the tap
To have a long nap

And wait for the next meal to come.

Nowhereland

walk with me.

Walk with ME.

Come along now.

This way.

Don't be scared,
Keep walking.

This road
leads to
Nowhere and Nothing.

Free from everything
and everyone
and nothing
and no one.

Nowhere
and Nothing
is empty and full
and it's this way
please come with me.

No wind.

No rain.

No light.

No dark.

No Me.

No You.

No more.

No less.

No today.

No tomorrow.

So walk with me
Walk with us
And find your place in Nowhere.

Warning!

Do Not Read

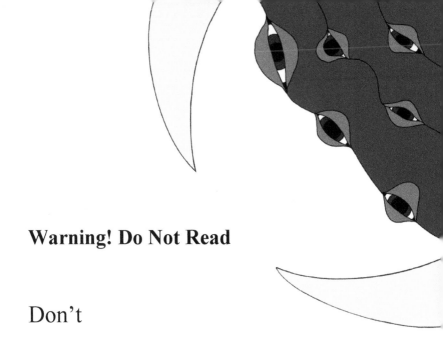

Warning! Do Not Read

Don't

Read

This

Poem

Carnivorous books draw people in
with small letters and rambling words
They close their spines on peoples' heads
as they're distracted by the blurbs

Blood Soaked Soles

Blood soaked soles
Eat your toes.

Flesh eating shoes
Chew.

Low / Near

Raindrops on the rooftop	PLOP
Trees that hit the glass panes	ROT
Creaks and squeaks of heaters	WHIR

&

People in the house	NO
	MORE
Quiet	AFTER
The	STORM

Daydream.

I had a dream in a day
      where roller coaster creatures play
with dripping pause and human eyes
      that burn and blister on the ride.
The cart then stops,
      creak idle on top.
It turns.
It waves.
It smiles.
It's grave.

Stuck in place,
Grin on its face,
      I'm stuck in time
      in the daydream of mine.

Marred Days

*

       *

   *

        *   *

           *

        *   *

*

*

*

The Suncatcher

jingle jangle
bead twine tangle
butterfly encrusted gem
sunshine dancing light again
rainbow beams that stick to tile
from lost houses bare and wild

*

*

*

*

Timestamps (It is Night)

It is Night

3:16 am

> There's a whooshing outside that's louder than usual on a still night.

3: 18 am

> I wake up with the haze of the still night stirring.

3:23 am

> I can't fall asleep so I get up to go to the bathroom down the hall facing the wood.

3:24 am

> I look outside the bathroom window into the darkness and there's a figure slithering through the air.

No wings, just a long winding body, back and forth,
flying directly towards the window.

Snake-like and white with bright yellow rounded
eyes and feathered face.

It slinks upward, elongating onto the branch
outstretched in front of me, towering and hovering
beyond the window.

Large and hooting it stares into my eyes.

I can't understand what it says.

But it stares and stares until I can't look anymore as
the giant figure looms in the darkness in front of me.

I won't go outside.

I won't open the window.

It should have had wings but the rounded feathered body slink slunks without propelling using the wind from the still night to land on the branch in front of me in the deadness of night to tell me nothing but silence and I do not understand but it's there and it stays and it stares at me in the dark steady night picturesque and substantial to take up most of my vision in the suburban woods of the backyard and no one else is here but the thing is here and it stares with the darkness but it's bright and obvious in the stealth of the night that I can't look at it as it stares at me with the body and the eyes and the beak and the feathers and the largeness and the slithering wingless features that stay floating silently in the night -

7:05 am

I wake up and go to the window.

Daytime and warm. The trees are light and the birds are chirping and nothing else moves but the leaves on the branches, but it was different last night and I still check the window to make sure nothing slithers toward the window in the brightness and warmness of day.

Marred Days

K. M. Jost

Birds of Prey

If Dinosaurs were here today
They'd disguise themselves as Birds of Prey
Swooping down while children play
To peck out eyes and fly away
Past the blood sky end of day
Leaving traceless winds to sway
The trees and leaves that blow

A W A Y

Concrete

Deep down under the earth
Dark room and flickering lights
Damp.

Concrete floors and restaurant chairs
Crusty pipe dripping
Cringe.

Glowing tank on the wall
Blue neon glow
Filter.

Footstep

        Footstep

    Footstep

Closer

The tank becomes clearer
Round and bulging eyes floating
Human glare and fish fins waving.

A connection.
It turns around
With grinning pearly white mouth -

Time to wake up now.
Not too late
To remember how.

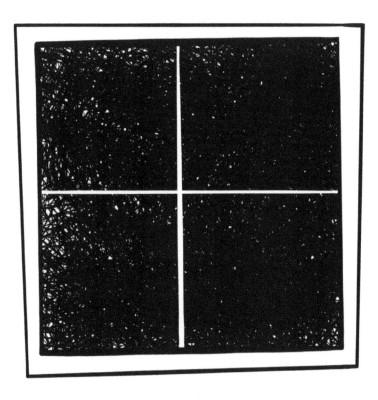

Of Icarus – Part 1

It was dark.

She opened her eyes
to the shadows draped across the walls,
watching the moonrise,
making patterns dance
      across the tattered walls.

It was lonely.

The corner lamp had been burnt out
for as long as she could remember,
hardly distinguishing that there ever
was a life
      outside the walls.

Her mind was empty,
closed off.

No emotions.
No ideas.

Marred Days

A rat scurried
across the floor
and hid under the stained grey couch
next to the lamp.

A few frayed wires,
jutting out from the cracks in the ceiling,
just low enough to graze
the top of her head when she stood.

A faint humming noise
from the next room,
followed by a series
of tin canned clicks.

As the humid night continued
to fog the dirty glass,
the sound slowly disintegrated,
signaling the end of testing for the day.

Emptiness of hissing gone,
she became aware of her breath.

It grew
        in wheezing patterns,
adding noise back into the foggy room,
sounding uneven and shattered;
mechanical in a sense.

It had been a long time

Days?

since she had last opened her mouth,
feeling the dryness
        and unclean taste,
she made her way to the sink,
kicking the dust and grime
with her feet along the way,
remaining silent with intent to stay unnoticed,
        like always.

Marred Days

One flickering oil lamp
above the faucet,
slowly dying out.

Not caring for light,
it faded away,
leaving only the moon's glare
to filter through the screen.

With a rusted spin,
the knob turned,
letting a thin brown liquid escape
into the cracked basin below.

It ran through the seams,
creating river tracks in a desert.

Reaching hands underneath,
the substance flowed over her skin
as if covered in wax.

The droplets rolled off her fingers
and dripped into the sink
like rainfall.

She watched the water stream
            down the drain,
not wondering where it went,
but knowing it would circulate back
to catch her skin once more out of the tap.

With a sip of unfiltered water,
she rinsed her dry mouth
and let the water return
            to its man-made path.

No breeze through the windows,
glass permanently installed.

The only air,
            hot,
entered through the ceiling vents,
where it then lay - stagnant.

Marred Days

Every now and then
a fan would be turned on,
mixing up the atmosphere
to a seemingly more pleasant arrangement,
but it would bring the dust up with it,
burying the room in a thin smoky layer
which ensured another night of
      difficult breathing.

This was all fine.

Whenever the air became too thick,
the shower would be turned on,
capturing the dust in steam,
forcing it back onto the ground

Whence It Came.

The room was small,
shower steam easily reaching the couch,
making it more bearable to live in
after the scent of soap was distributed throughout.

Her shower was a perk,
separated from the rest
for research purposes.

It kept her isolated
                    unharmed.

A few spots of mildew sprinkled on the bottom,
not enough to be harmful,
similar to the rest of the place.

A new bar of soap
dark yellow
had been placed on the rack
earlier that morning.

One towel
lay draped over the showerhead,
drying from earlier use,
but good enough to use again
now that it was nearly midnight.

Feeling awake
     and bored,
she stepped into the white shower,
turned the muddy water on to a warmer setting,
and began inspecting the same old stains
in the space above the plastic wall.

Her room was at the end of the space,
providing a long window to *out of* in the back.

Due to time
     or purpose,
it was lightly painted over
in a film of black paint
to dim the sunlight that could possibly find a way
     through.

On the opposite side of the couch,
a tripod with a camera perched on top.

It was pointed towards a white wall
with a metal folding chair facing the lens.

The dust in this portion of the room
was much less
than the rest,
for it had been used all day,
     and been used
          every day.

The seat was sagging
just enough
to notice a discomfort in the lower back
when sitting for more than five hours,
     which was
          often.

The recording
already collected
before sunset.

Twenty minutes
under the warmth of the shower.

Accepting that time was up,
she got out,
wrapped the damp towel around her body,
and sat on the lid of the toilet
      to comb her hair.

The new soap was friendlier,
but still left clumps of knots.

She sorted out the mess
and cleaned up the strands
forced onto the floor
from aggressive strokes.

It was still dark,
enough to be hidden from watching eyes,
so she snuck out of the bathroom
and changed into a pair of stretchy shorts
and a larger T-shirt
      provided by one of her male counterparts,
then settled back onto the worn cushions
where she slept.

K. M. Jost

As night crept on,
      the place was silent.

No sound of night bugs
or howling strays
could penetrate
      the steel walls.

No cars
or city sounds
could come close enough to the home
to make an impression.

In the silence
      and the darkness
           she began to doze off,
hearing faint ideas of another breath
from the other room
and feeling the surrounding of nothingness
barricade the entity from her world.

Probably Sick

Daytime fox
Prowls down the street
Gate bouncy
Fur thin
Foamed slimy wet grin.

Bubbles

pop

      pop

fizzle

      splash

Bubbles swirl around my bath

clink

      tink

drain

      whirr

Down the hole the water stirs

And if I sit
Upon the rim
I won't get pulled
Down deep within.

K. M. Jost

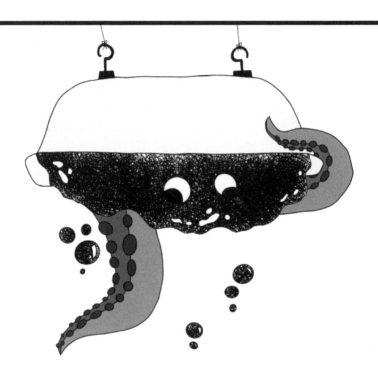

Halowell

A long green road
Between the ferns
Power lines overhead

She wanders between
On a street made of earth
With flower beds underfoot

A grate in the ditch
Of cement and iron
Checkered and locked from outside

A hitch in the latch
Rusted and weathered
The door is a gateway beyond

Crawling inside
Wet footsteps behind
Echoes into the dampness

No Cheshire meows
And the magic is missing
But the visions are just as enticing

Further into the swell
Where the rats dance with thistle
Below a graveyards' basement

Flowers of muck
Sunshine of sewage
A yellow brick road made of stench

The tunnel keeps going
And she follows it down
Because the window was open today.

House Pouse

The house pouse
Is not a mouse
Although it has a mouse-like snout.

Not *squeak*
But...

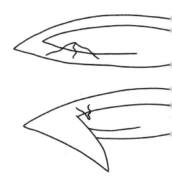

Ears

Fire so bright
Devil's delight
Heated brick oven
A crawlspace of cloven
hoofs from the Coven
Good night.

(42) Missed Calls

It's getting normal
To hear a DING
When objects want us to hear it.

But now that I'm home
In quiet alone,

I don't like the DING
When the telephone sings
For another voiceless missed call.

Shrink.

Why do shorts shrink in the winter?

Hibernating in the cold
Smaller and smaller from when they sold

A denim band so tight
It pinches in with all its might

The waistband sinks into the skin
And snaps in half a wearer less-thin

Distant

From me

To you
SIX

To you
THIRTEEN

No
More.

Attic

Attic door shakes.
Bottle hits floor.

breaks

Window smashes
Wind blown ashes

Down the stairs
E
S
C
E
N
D
I
N
G

Start of a
New ending.

K. M. Jost

Dulles Airport

In Dulles airport
The air is grey
The ports keep

shifting

One way
Another way

Locked door.
Opened door.

ALARM

And the planes go up
And out of sight
Into the clouds of the grey aired night.

Garden of Eaten

Front yard

Box

Growing envy

Rots

The plants tangled intertwines
With mushed organs under vines
To grab hold of little fingers
Picking through the leaf-like blisters

K. M. Jost

On the stem of edible blooms
That sink into corpse mud with molten fumes
Plumes on either side of muck
Bubbling up and down like suck

As He watches Her dive in
To leave him here where sin is sin
And she is free to swim again
Eaten by the Earth and End.

She will rise next season
With embers gleaming
From her eyes.

The Hedge

The cars were stopped in the usual line of traffic.

A traffic light hung on each crossroad,
keeping the factory line of commuters
steadily halted for the duration of the evening.

Heat poured into my van from the orange sun,
blinding my left eye as it drooped down from the sky.

One week, more, we've been in a heat wave.

Brown outs,
broken air conditioners,
a citywide shortage of fans and ice.

Four days prior
my car had begun whirring under the strain
and the air no longer cooled.

Letting the air blow in through my window,
stale gasoline steeped,
permeating from the dingy streets.

As we slowed into the inevitable gridlock,
the wind began to pick up.

Music echoed from the cars ahead.

In a world of creativity and art,
it is unexpectedly easy to overlook humanity.

In the peacefulness of stalled cars,
humanity is displayed in naturalness.

A private version of the selves
comes to surface after long days
of masks and
                    performances.

The businessmen sink into
either quiet reflection
or stress induced road rage.

Many times I've sat in the van,
windows down,
and the honking impatience of these businessmen
is inevitable.

To my right was a tall flowering hedge.

Ordinary.

In this neighborhood,
the hedges spread property across property,
keeping the outside out
        and the inside

                                in.

Life is separated by the hedge.

It grew tall,
covering the house behind it.

Despite the drought,
it had been watered regularly
as it was a lush green color
with floral blooms tangling around the vines.

Children walked by the hedge,
brushing their hands along the leaves,
rustling the border between them

                    and the others.

I watched them wander past the traffic,
going faster on foot,
living a carefree life
of laughter and summer freedom.

A breeze touched my cheek -
Hot and ethereal,
like something reaching through the veil
      and caressing.

The hedge rustled.

I looked.

The wind stopped.

The dead life of the cars
was muted by the heavy air,
dense and thick now.

My heart started fluttering.

In silence,
everything was slow.

Every movement
caused my eyes to shutter
        in and out of focus,
like a camera
trying to capture debris in a storm.

Empty,
no one walking down the street anymore
and the cars were locked in cement,
      yet the hedge was twitching
         with life.

More rustling,
no longer provoked by wind,
caused my eyes to shift focus
      to a cluster of shadow in the center of

                         it.

Pulsing and breathing,
the hedge began to form itself around my vision.

Black haze seeped from a wound in its core.

Slender and cut,
the wound slithered open
and howled a hollow wind.

Magnetic.

I tried to look around at the other people,
hoping to catch a glimpse of someone else
experiencing the same trance I was held in,
but the cars had vanished from the street.

Every road was now desolate,
and yet the traffic was still there,
stagnant gridlock invisible,
still holding me to the spot
        next to the hedge.

I fought.
I fought the wind
                and the force.

Grabbing the side of the rolled down window,
I clung to the car,
hoping to run
        in another direction.

But the shadow grew
     and grew
         and grew

           and pulled me under the car,
           dragging me into the rustling twigs
           that clattered like laughing cicadas.

Its breath was hot
and thick
like fresh tarmac on the road.

 It was alive

     and hungry

        and soon I was gone,

          eaten,

           and here.

Here is a new place.

It's blank.

There is nothing but aloneness and blankness.

The pit of the shadow is emptiness.

And I sit,
      here,
            somewhere,
                  forever.

Marred Days

K. M. Jost

Black and White and All Over

Tea cups chatter
Shatter
Glass across linoleum

Checker black and white
Sight
Wine stain zig zag patches

Bleach on wood

Stood

A man without reason

Breathing
Warmth and sweat
Eyes wet with regret
But it's done all the same

Marred Days

Neverending

S   p
  W   O
    0 o

s
 l
  i
   D
    E

R   a   i   d
D   g   R   e ⇉
    O n

Imaginary Friend

Her Smile is wide
Her teeth are chipped
And blood drips

d
O
w
n

Her finger TIPS

A Void

Windowless pain

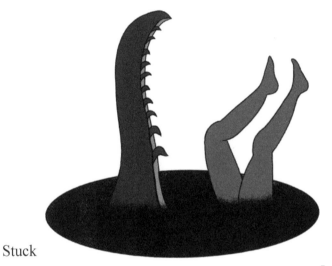

Stuck

In

Between

The inside:
Horror struck

Bad luck
Movie-esque scene

Remember to Forget

Molded pages
In the basement
Mildew smelling
Like cold damp bedding
For the spiders in the walls
Spindling webs in which they crawl
And fall onto heads of hair
Cleaning in forgotten air.

With stories and stories
Sitting on shelves
That haven't been read
Since before they were dead
But the moldy pages grow thicker
And the words smudge and fur
So the text can't be read
And they're laid down to bed.

Like this book someday
In your attic you may
Find it one day
And remember I say

The aging of words
That follow your time
May find their way back to you
Molded and blind
To the new world you live in
But that's the rhyme
And the reason it stands
Barely together by spine,
To bring past into present
And Life from the descent

So that your thoughts
can know Forgot.

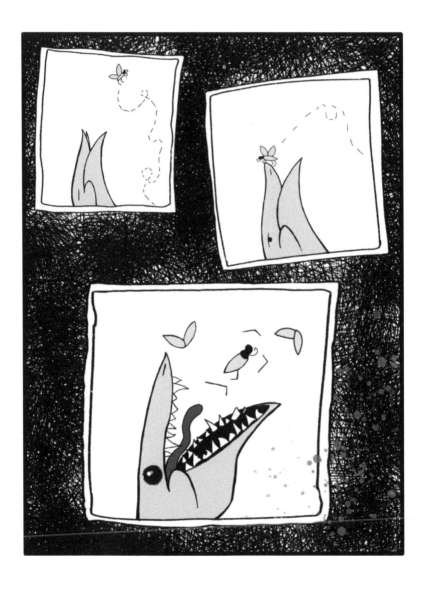

Ode to Humanity

Lord of the flies
With his big black eyes
Marching towards lies
With dusk on the rise

Bathing disguise
To fit in the size
Of all other guys
Who want to surmise

The truth
Of the situation.

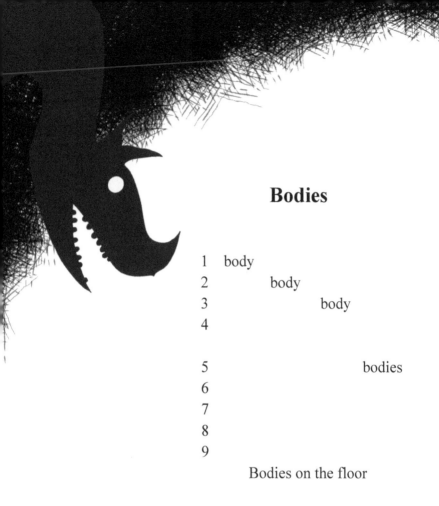

Bodies

1   body
2   body
3   body
4

5   bodies
6
7
8
9

Bodies on the floor

Small bodies
All bodies
Standing in the walls

Teeth clenched
Smile
Just like dolls.

asked and answered.

A question I have
For those who may know:

> *Where* does green grass grow?
> Why do days get *slow*?

In the pit of the fire
The burning Inquire
Lives at the start
And dies with the heart.

Burnt

Walk on the street
Small feet
Clattering
Pattering
Cobblestone lane
The same
Bell chimes seven
Heaven
Darkness plummets
Run it
Quick
Flick
Fire cascading on stone soaked road
Gasoline
Dreams
While the children scream
Awake in the night
No sight
Of relief

Through deepness and sleepless they go.

one

Morning Coffee

My coffee grounds smile at me
wink
blink   From   cup
See?   The   the
bottom of
A life I've now stirred up.

Hallways | Hallways

The hallway continued

Linoleum footsteps

And flickering bulbs in
my vision

A fridge full of milk jugs

Some fresh some rotting

By the staircase leading
both ways

Running,

Like always

But nowhere to get to

Endlessly circling

Rectangular prison

Hard soled shoes

Dead bugs spattered in the
shadow overhead.

Why was she there?

Big bushy hair.

Up and down, heaven and
hell.

Sweat

Every night, running

Where?

A pattern.

A mirror | A mirror
Doubled | Doubled
It was reflected only in one.

By looking through the glass
I saw
Another reflection beyond

Animated, Robotic, Real, and Plastic

Unblinking and hateful and matted and evil and raging and
waiting and seeing and breathing.

Two steps removed
But present at heart
Still | Behind
Beyond | The Barrier
The Mirror | Awake

DON'T
break.

Feed the Trees

They say that the trees listen.
If you walk alone in the forest, deep in the forest,
The trees hear your soul.

Every beating desire, that fire in your heart,
Breathes outward into the wind
And the leaves quiver with each exhale.

So don't wander into the den of trees
With a heavy heart
or guilt or greed -

K. M. Jost

Because the trees can hear
And they'll feed on your fear.

The trees will move
To create a trap
So you'll lose the path
And get lost in the wood
Like so many others did before.

two

If A Raven Could Speak

Telltale heart in the floor
Thump bumps, sure,
But when I'm no more
Does the thump get sore
Of thumping?

Or am I in my grave
Enslaved by chains,
To this thumping clump of gore?

Forevermore.

Indigestion

Gurgling stomach full of food
Swimming up and down.
The acid wanders up my throat
To take a look around.

The grumbling lump of human flesh
Had one too many bites.
Perhaps the time has come at last
To stop and say goodnight.

But here we are again, you see
The plumpy boilings shout.
Dinner pries at my insides
Just dying to come out.

Lost in Thought

There's a place I go

Where?

I don't know.

Deep within
Another mind perhaps?
Another life, foreign.

Thoughts swirl around
Hazy glitter and yesterdays,
Blinking a muted sound.

One step
         and the world shifts
Revolves, dissolved
The new canvas sits.

Drops of thoughts,
Old and future present,
Rorschach and Ink Blots

Create a world
In my mind
I find
When it decides to unfurl
like an uncurled curl
And carpet me inside.

afraid.

Sometimes fear
Is far and near.

A tickling of skin,
A breeze colder begins.

Shudder and shutter
Both loud in their own ways.

A presence,
Second sense,
Rickety fence,
Howls in the distance.

Sometimes fear is near and far,
But Nearer Fear is here
And No Fear is long gone.

friends

friends

Marred Days

To Greet Him as an Old Friend.

Last night - the sixth of December,
      not winter in the slightest.

I was walking through a field,
it was daytime.
Sunshine hitting the grass.
The warm air
 hanging, suspended,
      almost as if it were waiting for something.
I was with a girl,
    a quiet girl,
        inward.

She knew misery.
      And it followed her.
It followed us.

Three figures
    in the distance.
No mist for them to hide behind,
      yet they were cloaked and hidden from vision.

I could see every one of them clearly,
      for I was using different eyes than she.

The first,
      the most handsome,
      blonde hair,
      muscular,
      fit,
      and a genuine face,
           seemed anxious.

I wished for him to calm down.
It would be fine.
Why was he so worried?
It's okay - calm down.
Nothing's going to happen.

He glanced to another.

The next,
>   dark,
>   tall,
>   wider than the first.
>   A chiseled face.

He had a look of concentration about him.
He knew what he was here for.
He had to do it.
>   He had no choice.

I did not know.
>   We did not know.

The last,
>   the most skittish,
>   jittery, and ravenous.
>   Pale, with dark hair,
>   a sunken face,
>   piercing, and very thin, scarcely.

He was ready to attack.

Sprinting,
     Rabid,
          Rapid.
               He was unpredictable.

Then, I was in their heads.
     Listening to conversations yards away.

The second man was thinking.
He knows the girl is here.

Harm.
     Why?
          The third man wants to.
          He wants to run free,
          to cause disruption,
          violence.
               To kill.
          Good, she brought a friend,
          they all think alike.

They are all guilty.

But the one boy,
  the first boy - he knows of light.
    He knows of the living.

I turn.

He's next to me,
No longer enemy,
  but partner.

Two strangers in the Night, seeking Light.

I know. Trust me, I know.

He was one of them, but he was mine.

It's in his hand.
The blade looks tired,
  old,
    beaten.

The long wooden handle is worn in and faded, yet the
brilliance of this object was undeniable.
The glistening tip,
     so deadly,
          yet so tempting.
Every glint from this dazzling instrument allures.

So tempting, yes.

Here.
     One word.
This is the end of living.

Bloodthirsty, ready to kill.
And so quick -
     She is gone.
     Safe,
          out of the path of danger.

It happens.

One swing - so fast, so slow.
Stomach - slash.
Red life leaving.
Pain.
Not that of the axe.

A swing,
      not to kill,
            but to murder.

Neck sliced open.
Sharpened line of relief.
So precise,
      so little damage,
            yet so much red.

I wake.
      Clean.
      Sanitized?
I smelt the empty whiteness of the room.
I was out of place.

Remember the axe?
 The torture.

        Stop.

It slowly subdued to a dull numbness.

But there was a pain
        deeper.

        My heart.
                aching.
                crying.
                Why?
                        It knew no such pain.

Gasping for breath.

                Suffocating, air!

        Stop.
It kept on.

It urged to go on,
but I begged for it to stop.

Stop!

It did not listen.

It merely ran faster into burning flames.

Stop!

It sped into a chaos of turning, punching, bleeding, STOP! I
begged! I pleaded!

It never stopped.

It kept lurching for life, for something I could not give!
Still, every beat cries.

It would not stop.

He was there again.
In the dark cloak that leads to light.
Sleep, he said.
So quietly,
so soothingly.

You too, I said.
And I slept.

Messy thing to do, that.

The world was still in motion, so we went on.
The horror we have faced, is masked for the world.
A show not for the faint of heart.

And so we find the light

That two strangers shared in the night.

Marred Days

Memories Lost

Cushioned pillow
on my chair
I'm
  "not all there"
    they say.

Crocheted patterns
  learned,
  forgotten,
In the far-off times of   yesterday.

Marred Days

Swan

Cold.
The wind begins to stir round.
Face, hidden.
Chills run down arms, and hair whips in and out of place.
But we are calm.

Ready.

Snow is falling on the freshly frozen surface,
Slips of ice forming slick.
Another gust.

People, the normal people walk to their car.
We don't need them.
We don't need them to see us now.

Turn back around and hear them leave.
Alone once more.
The sun is almost down now, and then it will be time.
The gates sway, and the creaks of the rusted metal cringe.
The sun takes one last breath, and dives.

Tree Fiend

While trees are moving,
bouncing, swaying,
because the wind is blowing,

Me,

I tunnel underground,
round and round,
and further down,

to cut and break their roots.

Night Wanderer

The cool autumn rush of crisp air whips by,
and I think of you.

My mind lingers on yours,
for you are indecipherable.
Incomprehensible.
Intriguing.
In love.

　　　I am.

　　　　　with you.

So much like the insanity building in me,
The fate of us is not a question.

There is no fate,
yet I cannot deny.

What I feel does not subside,
and for if it does not I near cry,
and wane with the moon.

Until eclipse covers mine heart.
Until it has again become dark.

In moonlight, in the night, the stars shine welcome.

A map to forever. Wandering.

Inside Counts

U
N

Z
I
p

M
E

I'm stuffed with fluff.

Of Icarus - Part 2

The screech of the morning bell
calls out across the center,
bursts of static interrupting
From the ancient amplification system
built for what was once a school.

Daggers of neon orange
rupture through the smallest of specks
missing and worn off
in the black tinted window.

The kind of light
that comes with the apocalypse,
      unforgiving and deadly.

She knows better
than to sleep beyond the hour,
a minute too long
and the ray would crawl across the room,
like a beam of energy
      destroying any life along the way.

Marred Days

The breathing
in the next room
is refreshed and waiting.

It responds to a new day,
a new chance at success.

The old tales were right
      about the calling,
           the needing.

Still mechanical,
it sharpens at her movement,
hoping to latch on once more.

At this,
the static bell transforms into fuzzy sentences,
calling out the duties for the day.

Step one,
>   enter your holding chamber.
Step two,
>   latch.
Step three,
>   One.

She does as told,
as she does every day,
as she has done every day
>   for as long as she can remember.

She was bred for this.

In the holding chamber
the air excites.

No longer a stagnant night,
but a sweltering day.

Here,
the temperature is lower,
cooled by the insulation.

A necessity for it to live.

Grey brick walls,
tiled floor,
remnants -
an emergency eyewash station
     in the corner complete with a drain underfoot.

Stationed,
    on display,
       resting,
          in the center of the room
A pair of wings,
slowly moving in
    and out
as if wrapped around a ribcage.

Hum and Pump
in the rhythm of a dog
seeing the leash taken out.

Time to go outside,
time to go.

Protocol is announced
          yet again.

Stand on the line,
state your name,
date,
and trial case.

Wait for the invitation.
So she does exactly that.

> Name: #006
> Date: Day 7665
> Trial: Of Ikaros

Marred Days

On her affirmation
the wings unfurl,
glittering with the flecks of dust around the room.

No more cracks
      or dents
from the day before,
these wings have crusted over
with a new layer,
just like her skin.

They are One after all.

She steps up to the platform
encasing the wings
and greets them.

Linking like a wax seal,
they bond;
two life forms coming together,
      symbiosis.

The real ones -
restored from the lump that washed ashore,
and she -
the created descendent.

Meant to be together,
they embrace,
and steady themself for the routine.

They can feel it,
a new sense of together,
unlike any day before.

The countdown begins:
       five,
              four,
                     three,
                           two,
                                  One
- and the gate comes out from under them.

Falling into blackness,
falling, not flying.

Farther and farther
into the depths of the center
until the next gate opens up
and the upside down becomes right side up
and they fly up higher and higher
        away from the sea.

Beneath them
the water parts from another trial,
a glint of trident sparkles from afar.

Further up
the lightning grows stronger
and the limits of their flight have been reached.

Gliding down,
they see the sun outside the container,
squeaking light through the glass,
enough to point out the direction.

They are One,
and One wants to feel the warmth.

This is how it happened last time,
a taste of warmth
and a desire
        and a needing.

All the days before,
she could fight it,
but not today,
today was different.

It roars with anger
and pulls them towards the glass,
dragging them higher until they reach it -
the barrier that is meant to keep them safe.

Safe
        and imprisoned.

Now it has a body,
it has muscle,
to break free of this cell.

There is no stopping it.

Beating after beating
on the glass,
her ragged form
bloodied and wrecked dangles below the wings.

One hair thin crack streaks across the glass.

Barely any life left in her,
it uses their last strength
clawing away at the seam,
ripping open a gap
       wide enough to shred the last of her away.

And as she falls to the ocean,
it soars towards the sun.

Lost once more.

Marred Days

The Wrong Path

The flame dances on my palm, and I see the life I want.
Free.

The water floods and crashes in.

When two diverge - I took the one less traveled.
How was I to know it was the wrong road?

The daisies bloom in search of light,
But ivy thrives at darkest night.

The path unworn may creep the soul,
But treaded path will lead no gold.

If, however, two collide,
the moon would show the life divide.

Follow heart's intentions best,
But sit for none of mind's requests.

Tricks and turns unset the world,
So take the time nor need be told.

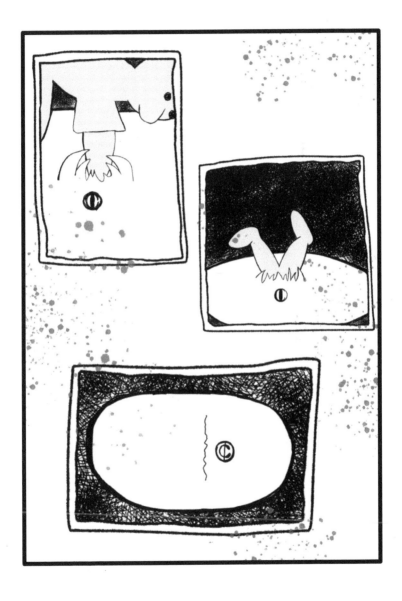

Wind Wisps.

Bed of flowers
Bed of thorns
I walk upon your sheets

Tucked neatly
In your earthen covers
Gentle firm and love

Prickled petals scratch
And tickle
The skin upon my neck

Wind wisps
Carving little smiles
Into warming drips

Into dust
A cozy nest
Decaying for what's next.

K. M. Jost

Crossing

I was following the long road home.
Brown and dusk setting around me.
The leaves were scattered,
News of the coming change
And I could feel the day leaving for tomorrow.

A new moon rose, silent and unglowing as ever.
Non-luminescent night descended around,
Making mysteries of the path.
Creaks and branches stuck out harsher than before
And I could feel the breeze turning colder.

Longingly, my pace quickened to get home
Each step clanging out in the blackness
A sharp inhale broke my stride and I collapsed at its feet
And I could feel the darkness closing around me.

"Why do you travel through the lightless night?"
It asked.

Feathers tucked neatly into the darkness around it.
Only the glint of sheen to make it out.

"With no light there is no tomorrow,
So why not go back to today?"

My eyes deceived me as I began to take in his breadth.
Claws like tree roots and beak curved around a tree trunk,
It was one with the night
And it saw where I was going.

I was unable to speak,
So I held out my arms,
A symbol of my decision to travel.

It broke the veil
And chose my fate for me,
Bloody and lifeless it came,
And I could feel the embrace of the night.

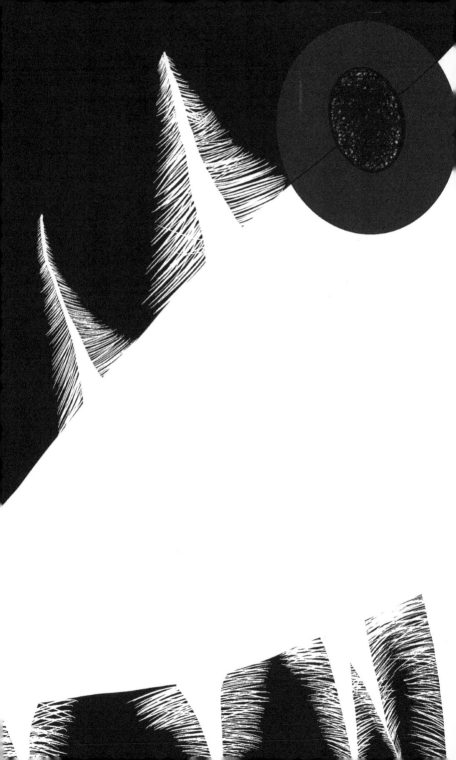

K. M. Jost

For 11

He was there. Next to me.

> jaws clenched
> salivating

And I could hear his little breathing,
Bits of life in and out,

> drops of hunger hit the ground

His tiny world, my orbit.

> marked and chosen
> steps of drowsy footsteps sound

But without a sound
A crashing comet
Impacts my Earth in silent destruction

> grab the fawn

And the little lights are lost.

A secret locked in this forest,
For now, for tomorrow, until that day.
That day when impact becomes explosion
And the planet either resolves revolving
Or fragments from despair.

> in Dusk we hide
> our prey til Dawn

Marred Days

Marred Days

When you look out the window of a moving car
And see the world in front of you -

The twists and turns of roadside beauty
Quiet humming meditation,

Figures only seen in night
Tiptoe in your brain
And make you see all kinds of things
Reserved for nightmare terrors.

Whispering comments in your ear speak of
Imaginary accidents where
Living statues pierce your soul and
Tremors in your core.

These nightmare daymares come to life
When we least expect.

No sunshine keeps the thoughts away.

We all have marred days ahead.

kmjost.com

CPSIA information can be obtained
at www.ICGtesting.com
Printed in the USA
LVHW070047230421
685283LV00023B/1517

9 781087 950723